Play

Presents
Shakespeare's

As You Like It

FOR KIDS
(The melodramatic version!)

For 7-17 actors, or kids of all ages who want to have fun!
Creatively modified by
Brendan P. Kelso
Cover stage illustrated by Shana Hallmeyer
Cover Characters by Ron Leishman

3 Melodramatic Modifications of Shakespeare's Play
for 3 different group sizes:

7-10 Actors

9-12 Actors

12-17+ Actors

Table Of Contents

To Rosie,
who, like Rosalind, is funny, beautiful,
brilliant, bold, fiercely independent,
and full of wonderful energy!

-Dad

Playing with Plays™ - Shakespeare's As You Like It for Kids

Copyright © 2004-2020 by Brendan P. Kelso, Playing with Plays LLC
Some characters on the cover are ©Ron Leishman ToonClipart.com

For performance rights please see page 6 of this book or contact:

contact@PlayingWithPlays.com

-Please note, for certain circumstances, we do waive copyright and performance fees. Rules subject to change

www.PlayingWithPlays.com

Printed in the United States of America
Published by Playing With Plays LLC

ISBN: 9781072660972

Foreword

When I was in high school there was something about Shakespeare that appealed to me. Not that I understood it mind you, but there were clear scenes and images that always stood out in my mind. Romeo & Juliet, "Romeo, Romeo; wherefore art thou Romeo?"; Julius Caesar, "Et tu Brute"; Macbeth, "Double, Double, toil and trouble"; Hamlet, "to be or not to be"; A Midsummer Night's Dream, all I remember about this was a wickedly cool fairy and something about a guy turning into a donkey that I thought was pretty funny. It was not until I started analyzing Shakespeare's plays as an actor that I realized one very important thing, I still didn't understand them. Seriously though, it's tough enough for adults, let alone kids. Then it hit me, why don't I make a version that kids could perform, but make it easy for them to understand with a splash of Shakespeare lingo mixed in? And voila! A melodramatic masterpiece was created! They are intended to be melodramatically fun!

THE PLAYS: There are 3 plays within this book, for three different group sizes. The reason: to allow educators or parents to get the story across to their children regardless of the size of their group. As you read through the plays, there are several lines that are highlighted. These are actual lines from the original book. I am a little more particular about the kids saying these lines verbatim. But the rest, well... have fun!

The entire purpose of this book is to instill the love of a classic story, as well as drama, into the kids.

And when you have children who have a passion for something, they will start to teach themselves, with or without school.

These plays are intended for pure fun. Please DO NOT have the kids learn these lines verbatim, that would be a complete waste of creativity. But do have them basically know their lines and improvise wherever they want as long as it pertains to telling the story. Because that is the goal of an actor: to tell the story. In A Midsummer Night's Dream, I once had a student playing Quince question me about one of her lines, "but in the actual story, didn't the Mechanicals state that 'they would hang us'?" I thought for a second and realized that she had read the story with her mom, and she was right. So I let her add the line she wanted and it added that much more fun, it made the play theirs. I have had kids throw water on the audience, run around the audience, sit in the audience, lose their pumpkin pants (size 30 around a size 15 doesn't work very well, but makes for some great humor!) and most importantly, die all over the stage. The kids love it.

One last note: if you want some educational resources, loved our plays, want to tell the world how much your kids loved performing Shakespeare, want to insult someone with our Shakespeare Insult Generator, or are just a fan of Shakespeare, then hop on our website and have fun:

PlayingWithPlays.com

With these notes, I'll see you on the stage, have fun, and break a leg!

SCHOOL, AFTERSCHOOL, and SUMMER classes

I've been teaching these plays as afterschool and summer programs for quite some time. Many people have asked what the program is, therefore, I have put together a basic formula so any teacher or parent can follow and have melodramatic success! As well, many teachers use my books in a variety of ways. You can view the formula and many more resources on my website at: PlayingWithPlays.com

- Brendan

OTHER PLAYS AND FULL LENGTH SCRIPTS

We have over **25** different titles, as well as a full-length play in 4-acts for theatre groups: Shakespeare's Hilarious Tragedies. You can see all of our other titles on our website here: PlayingWithPlays.com/books

As well, you can see a sneak peek at some of those titles at the back of this book.

And, if you ever have any questions, please don't hesitate to ask at: Contact@PlayingWithPlays.com

ROYALTIES

If you have any questions about royalties or performance licenses, here are the basic guidelines:

1) Please contact us! We always LOVE to hear about a school or group performing our books! We would also love to share photos and brag about your program as well! (with your permission, of course)

2) If you are a group and DO NOT charge your kids to be in this production, contact us about discounted copyright fees (one way or another, we will make this work for you!) You are NOT required to buy a book per kid (but, we will still send you some really cool Shakespeare tattoos for your kids!)

3) If you are a group and DO charge your kids to be in the production, (i.e. afterschool program, summer camp) we ask that you purchase a book per kid. Contact us as we will give you a bulk discount (10 books or more) and send some really cool press on Shakespeare tattoos!

4) If you are a group and DO NOT charge the audience to see the plays, please see our website FAQs to see if you are eligible to waive the performance royalties (most performances are eligible).

5) If you are a group and DO charge the audience to see the performance, please see our website FAQs for performance licensing fees (this includes performances for donations and competitions).

Any other questions or comments, please see our website or email us at:

contact@PlayingWithPlays.com

The 15-Minute or so As You Like It

By William Shakespeare
Creatively modified by
Brendan P. Kelso

7 - 10 Actors

CAST OF CHARACTERS:

ROSALIND (later Ganymede): our heroine! And Duke Senior's daughter

CELIA (later Aliena): Rosalind's best friend; Duke Fredrick's daughter

[3]**TOUCHSTONE:** a clown who is funny

[1]**DUKE FREDRICK:** rotten duke who took Duke Senior's throne

[3]**DUKE SENIOR:** happily lives in the woods with his merry men

OLIVER: Orlando's terrible older brother

ORLANDO: Oliver's younger brother; LOVES Rosalind

[2]**CHARLES:** kingdom's wrestler (think WWE!)

[1]**JAQUES:** a melancholy man (with a FAMOUS speech)

[2]**AUDREY:** loves Touchstone

The same actors can play the following part:

[1]DUKE FREDRICK and JAQUES
[2]AUDREY and CHARLES
[3]TOUCHSTONE and DUKE SENIOR can be doubled. BUT, Touchstone and Audrey's lines, in the last act, need to be removed.

Located at the back of the book is a simple pronunciation key for the names and some words throughout the play.

ACT 1 SCENE 1
ORCHARD OF OLIVER'S HOUSE

(enter ORLANDO addressing audience)

ORLANDO: I am soooo bummed. Why, you ask? Well, Dad died AND he left ALL his money to my older brother, Oliver. *(pauses and looks at audience member)* You don't get it, do you? Oliver DESPISES me and won't send me to school! I will no longer endure it! Here comes my snot-nosed brother now.

(enter OLIVER)

OLIVER: Well, if it's not my stinking little brother.

ORLANDO: I deserve my inheritance!

OLIVER: You deserve to live in the barn, Orlando!

ORLANDO: Aghhh! I've had it!!! *(they fight; ORLANDO is holding OLIVER)*

OLIVER: LET ME GO!!!

ORLANDO: Not until I get my money!

OLIVER: FINE!! *(ORLANDO lets go)* I pray you leave me. No one loves you anyway!!!

(ORLANDO exits; enter CHARLES)

OLIVER: Charles! How's life being the kingdom's wrestler?

CHARLES: Good. But, I have BIG news!

OLIVER: Yes? Do tell!

CHARLES: *(addressing audience and Oliver)* Well, Duke Fredrick just kicked his older brother, Duke Senior, out of the kingdom and usurped his throne!

OLIVER: You burped?

CHARLES: No! Usurped... he stole it!

OLIVER: Oh, fancy word. Go on.

CHARLES: So, Duke Senior now lives in the Forest of Arden with a band of merry men.

OLIVER: So... they live like Robin Hood?

CHARLES: Yes!

OLIVER: What about their daughters?

CHARLES: Rosalind, Duke Senior's daughter, is allowed to stay because she is best friends with Celia, Duke Fredrick's daughter.

OLIVER: Wow, nice exposition. It's almost as if you're setting the whole story up for the audience.

CHARLES: Exactly! But, I have a problem.

OLIVER: Really?

CHARLES: Yes. Your brother wants to fight me, the Great Charles, *(showing his muscles)* at the palace.

OLIVER: *(to audience)* Opportunity!

CHARLES: But, I'm gonna kick his butt, and it'll make me look bad... beating a nobleman.

OLIVER: *(with a bit of an evil snicker)* Oh, no, no, no, my friend! Orlando is cunning and deceitful and will use poison or entrap thee by some treacherous device. You need to crush him! No... SMASH him to pieces!

CHARLES: Smash?

OLIVER: Yes, smash, Charles. SMASH!

CHARLES: Charles, smash!!!

OLIVER: That's the spirit!

(ALL exit; CHARLES is repeating, "Charles, smash!")

ACT 1 SCENE 2
DUKE FREDRICK'S PALACE

(enter CELIA and ROSALIND)

CELIA: I pray thee, Rosalind, sweet my coz, be merry.

ROSALIND: If you can teach me how to forget a banished father, then I'll be merry.

CELIA: Tell ya what, when my father dies, I'll give you the kingdom back. Therefore, my dear Rose, be merry!

ROSALIND: Cool! I'm bored. I know! What think you of falling in love?

CELIA: Sounds like fun! *(enter TOUCHSTONE)* Well, hello clown, how are you today?

TOUCHSTONE: Joke: What was the nickname for the knight who ruled the fort? Fortnight!

ROSALIND: Ha ha! *(pauses)* I don't get it.

TOUCHSTONE: You know, fort-knight... aghh, nevermind. Here come the Duke and the wrestlers.

(enter DUKE FREDRICK, CHARLES, and ORLANDO)

DUKE F: How now, daughter and niece, here to see the wrestling?

CELIA: Yep!

ROSALIND: *(to ORLANDO)* Hey, that guy's pretty strong. Are you sure you want to get your butt kicked?

ORLANDO: *(warming up and not noticing ROSALIND)* Me? Hah! I will beat him with the strength of my youth! *(poses)*

CELIA: You know, this is the perfect time to panic and run.

ORLANDO: Bah! My brother detests me and I have little money, so I have nothing left to lose. Let's rumble!

DUKE F: *(addresses audience)* Ladies and gentlemen! In this corner, Charles the Magnificent! *(EVERYONE cheers)* and in this corner... *(to ORLANDO)* Uh... what's your name, kid?

ORLANDO: *(thinks)*... Captain O!

DUKE F: Captain O? K, he's going to get smashed!!! *(ROSALIND and CELIA cheer)*

CHARLES: Charles, SMASH!!!

ROSALIND: Now Hercules be thy speed, young man!

(they wrestle and ORLANDO wins)

DUKE F: What is thy name, young man?

ORLANDO: Orlando, my liege.

DUKE F: As in Sir Roland's son? My enemy? Humph!!! Now I'm mad! Let's leave.

(DUKE F exits)

ORLANDO: I am proud to be Sir Roland's son.

ROSALIND: My father loved Sir Roland.

ORLANDO: *(stunned by ROSALIND'S beauty)* Ahhh... wow... ohhh...

CELIA: *(pats ORLANDO on the back)* Well said, Captain O. Shall we go, coz?

ROSALIND: Hey, you're kinda cute.

ORLANDO: Ahhh...ohhh...

ROSALIND: Fare you well.

(CELIA and ROSALIND exit)

ORLANDO: *(to audience)* What passion hangs these weights upon my tongue? *(mocking himself)* Ahhhh... ohhhh... I'm such a fool! But, I gotta go! From tyrant duke unto a tyrant brother, how fun! But, heavenly Rosalind!

(ALL exit)

ACT 1 SCENE 3

DUKE FREDRICK'S PALACE

(enter CELIA and ROSALIND)

ROSALIND: Oh, Orlando!

CELIA: Cheer up, the play just started. I'm SURE we will see him again! But, here comes my dad with his eyes full of anger.

(enter DUKE FREDRICK)

DUKE F: *(to ROSALIND)* You! You're out of my kingdom! Okay, bye!

ROSALIND: Wait, what.. huh?! But why?

DUKE F: You like that Orlando guy and I trust thee not. Thou art thy father's daughter, there's enough.

CELIA: *(steps forward)* But daddy...

DUKE F: *(to CELIA)* STOP! Open not thy lips. She is banished.

(DUKE F exits)

CELIA: AHHHH!!! I'm soooo mad! *(screams offstage towards DUKE F)* Father, seek another heir! You banished her and hath banished me!

ROSALIND: Wow, that was dramatic. Where shall we go?

CELIA: The Forest of Arden to find your dad.

ROSALIND: The forest? We have to be careful, beauty provoketh thieves sooner than gold.

CELIA: Then, we'll disguise ourselves!

ROSALIND: Great idea! I'll dress as a man, as Jove's own page, Ganymede.

CELIA: And I'll be a poor shepherd girl.

ROSALIND: Why?

CELIA: Because I can! Now, to liberty, and not to banishment!

ROSALIND & CELIA: Yeah!

(ALL exit)

ACT 2 SCENES 1 & 2

THE FOREST AND THE PALACE

(enter DUKE SENIOR on one side of stage; enter DUKE FREDRICK on the other; they are in separate scenes but juxtaposed on stage; they address the audience)

DUKE S: I LOVE country life. Fresh air, beautiful trees, quiet streams, and peaceful animals.

DUKE F: I LOVE being the duke! Ruling everyone and my lords groveling to me. Speaking of which, where's my servant?! *(yelling offstage)* Someone grovel to me!!!

OFFSTAGE VOICE: You are most magnificent, your grace!

DUKE F: That's better!

DUKE S: You know, I do love teasing melancholy Jaques! He is always such a downer! Come! Let's have some fun!

(DUKE SENIOR exits; note flies onto stage)

DUKE F: *(picks up note)* Ah, must be more praise for the great me! *(reading)* Rosalind, your daughter, and the clown, have all left the kingdom to look for Duke Senior and to find Orlando. *(to audience)* WHAT the what!?!? I need to find Orlando's brother, Oliver! *(starts leaving)* NOW!!! *(offstage we hear, "yes sir!!!")*

(DUKE F exits)

ACT 2 SCENE 3

BEFORE OLIVER'S HOUSE

(enter ORLANDO addresses audience)

ORLANDO: So, rumor has it that my brother, Oliver, is planning on killing me. Well, I've got nothin' left here, so, I'm going to run off into the forest. Bye!

(ORLANDO exits)

ACT 2 SCENE 4

FOREST OF ARDEN

(enter ROSALIND [Ganymede], and CELIA [Aliena], and TOUCHSTONE)

ROSALIND: How weary are my spirits. Finally, we are here. This is the Forest of Arden.

TOUCHSTONE: I have no spirits, my legs hurt. *(lays down)*

CELIA: I cannot go any further. Touchstone, tell me a joke.

TOUCHSTONE: Knock, knock.

CELIA: Who's there?

TOUCHSTONE: No one! I'm too tired to answer! *(pretends to sleep)*

CELIA: Silly fool.

ROSALIND: Come on, let's find my dad and that cute Orlando guy.

CELIA: Great! Maybe I'll find love too!

TOUCHSTONE: Blah... I'm sure everyone would love me, too, but I can't force everyone to have good taste now, can I?

CELIA: Come on, fool.

TOUCHSTONE: Yes, let's search for love, because, love is all you need... that and a good cup of coffee!

(ALL exit)

THE FOREST

(enter JAQUES; offstage someone is singing some simple country song)

JAQUES: *(yelling)* Quit singing that dreadful song! *(to audience)* Oh, hello. Question. WHO, in their right mind, would leave riches to move to the woods. *(yelling offstage)* You're all demented! *(to audience)* I'm randomly walking off in search of nothing. See ya!

(JAQUES exits; enter DUKE SENIOR)

DUKE S: *(to audience)* Have you seen Jaques? *(pauses as he seems to interact with audience to find JAQUES)* No? Yes? That way? Thanks! *(enter JAQUES)* Ah, Jaques. I was just looking for you.

JAQUES: *(very happy)* HELLO!

DUKE S: What, you look merrily! Very unlike you.

JAQUES: A fool, a fool! I met a fool i' the forest. I WANT to be a fool! I found my life's calling!

DUKE S: You do realize we already think you're a fool? Plus, the play already has a fool, so...

JAQUES: Whatever.

(ORLANDO enters brandishing sword)

ORLANDO: Forbear and eat no more, or I will have to kill you all! In other words, gimmie food or die!

DUKE S: Food? Is that all? Well then, come and join us.

ORLANDO: Really? Cool.

JAQUES: *(addresses everyone)* Did you know...

All the world's a stage,

And all the men and women merely players:

They have their exits and their entrances;

And one man in his time plays many parts,

His acts being seven ages. At first the infant,

Mewling and puking...

ORLANDO: Gross! We're eating here!

DUKE S: There goes my appetite...

JAQUES: Fine! *(JAQUES exits)*

DUKE S: Hey, aren't you the good Sir Roland's son, my old friend?

ORLANDO: Yes.

DUKE S: Well, welcome to the tribe!

ORLANDO: Sweet!

(ALL exit)

ACT 3 SCENE 1

A ROOM IN THE PALACE

(enter DUKE F and OLIVER)

DUKE F: You!

OLIVER: Yes, sir!

DUKE F: I need you to find and kill your brother, or I kill you, capisce? *(pronounced Kuh-PEESH)*

OLIVER: Of course! I never loved my brother in my life.

DUKE F: Good! Now get out of here! *(OLIVER runs off; to audience)* Wow, I love being powerful!!!

(DUKE F exits)

THE FOREST

(for the rest of the play)

(enter ORLANDO, leaving poems lying around)

ORLANDO: *(to audience)* Oh, my heart!!! My achy-breaky heart! I LOVE Rosalind sooooo much that I'm leaving random poems scattered throughout the forest. Here, have some... go on, read it to all... *(audience member reads, it's TERRIBLE)* Oh... isn't it WONDERFUL?! *(exits dancing happily)*

(enter ROSALIND [Ganymede], CELIA [Aliena], and TOUCHSTONE)

ROSALIND: *(picks up a poem)* What's this? *(reads)* "From the east to the western Ind; No jewel is like Rosalind." Ahhh, how cute.

TOUCHSTONE: Oh, garbage I say... *(in a mocking voice)*

Oh, I'm a fool!

Look at me drool,

Over some girl,

BLEH! Makes me want to hurl!

CELIA: Oh quiet, Touchstone! You'll find love to be awesome one day, too!

TOUCHSTONE: Never! *(exits)*

CELIA: I think I know who wrote these. *(reads another aloud)* "Rosalind is beautiful, and my love is suitable... for her." Wow, these are terrible...

ROSALIND: True. Wait, what?! You know... WHO?!!!

CELIA: Well, I'm not sure...

ROSALIND: But who is it?!!! *(rambles)* What does he look like? Will I like him? Is he ugly?

CELIA: Well...

ROSALIND: *(continuing right over CELIA)* What if he's short? Or he doesn't shower? Or has a mustache? Ewww... Wait... What if he's THE ONE?

CELIA: Well, this IS a romantic comedy...

ROSALIND: *(continuing to ramble)* Can I get my father to approve? Why is this confusing? Are you pulling my leg? Is that gas I'm feeling? Who gave me coffee? Did you write these?

CELIA: What? Yes. No. STOP! No... aghhh... you ask too many questions!

ROSALIND: Do you not know I am a woman? When I think, I must speak!

CELIA: Sheesh! It is young Orlando, that doofus wrestling guy we met.

ROSALIND: Oh... *(suddenly realizing)* OHHHH... HIM.... Oh, he's dreamy...

CELIA: Yes "him"... and look, here "him" is now...

(enter ORLANDO and JAQUES, laughing)

ORLANDO: No, you're Monsieur Melancholy.

JAQUES: Stop it, Signior Love.

ORLANDO: Am not! Ok, I am...

(JAQUES exits)

ROSALIND: You are what?

ORLANDO: In love... wait, who are you?

ROSALIND: The name is Ganymede.

ORLANDO: Gany-who?

ROSALIND: Nevermind. *(to CELIA)* I'm going to speak to him like a saucy lackey and play the knave with him.

CELIA: What, was that even English?

ROSALIND: It means, I'm going to mess with him.

CELIA: Oh!

ROSALIND: *(to ORLANDO)* We were laughing at some lovesick lunatic who was going around carving the name, "Rosalind" on all the trees.

ORLANDO: That be me that is so love-shaked! Do you have a remedy for this feeling?

ROSALIND: I can cure you of this lovesickness.

ORLANDO: Really? How?

ROSALIND: I will pretend I'm this... uh... this Rosalind and you will come every day and woo me.

ORLANDO: What? You're a dude, and you look NOTHING like my fair Rosalind.

ROSALIND: Nothing? Really? Are you sure? Maybe the lighting is off... anyway, pretend, and I will cure you of your lovesick lunacy!

ORLANDO: This is confusing.

ROSALIND: This is Shakespeare, just do it.

ORLANDO: With all my heart, good youth, I'll do as you say.

ROSALIND: And don't call me 'good youth', call me Rosalind!

ORLANDO: As you like it! *(to audience)* Get it?

(ALL exit)

ACT 4 SCENE 1

(enter ROSALIND [Ganymede] and CELIA [Aliena]; pause then enter ORLANDO)

ORLANDO: Good day, dear Rosalind.

ROSALIND: Don't 'good day' me! You're late!

ORLANDO: I'm only an hour late.

ROSALIND: Break an hour's promise in love? Then you don't love at all!

ORLANDO: But...

ROSALIND: Get out of here and try this again! *(ORLANDO waits, confused)* Go!

(ORLANDO exits then re-enters)

ORLANDO: Ok, I'm back!

ROSALIND: That's not how you greet a love! Go! Do it again! If you want Rosalind to love you, then you need to WOOOO her! Now go! Come back a better woo-er!

(CELIA shoves ORLANDO off stage; ORLANDO re-enters)

ORLANDO: My dear, Rosalind...

ROSALIND: *(interrupting)* Better... Now, come, woo me, woo me.

ORLANDO: Ok... I love you.

ROSALIND: *(mocking ORLANDO)* I love you... blah, blah, blah... you do not love. Show me LOVE!

ORLANDO: I die for love and I would die for you!

ROSALIND: Better. But, you saw what happened to Romeo & Juliet, dying for love may not be the best thing. I got it! Aliena, act as a priest and marry us!

CELIA: *(shocked)* What?!

ROSALIND: Priest, you know... marriage! Just do it!

CELIA: Okey-dokey. *(they hold hands)* Will you, Orlando, have to wife this Rosalind?

ORLANDO: I will. I take thee, Rosalind, for a wife.

ROSALIND: *(feeling love-struck)* Wow. Ok, you're doing great!

ORLANDO: But, will my Rosalind do so?

ROSALIND: By my life, she will do as I do! *(to audience)* Really, she will!

ORLANDO: O, but she is wise!

ROSALIND: *(to audience)* Very true! *(to ORLANDO)* Now, get out of here and don't be late again!

ORLANDO: Aye, sweet Rosalind. Adieu! *(exits)*

CELIA: Wow, you really got him in shape!

ROSALIND: *(sighs heavily)* I know...

CELIA: *(pulling ROSALIND offstage)* Come on crazy Cupid.

(ALL exit)

ACT 4 SCENE 2

(enter AUDREY and TOUCHSTONE)

TOUCHSTONE: Hey, you're cute.

AUDREY: Ahhh... thanks!

TOUCHSTONE: I have an idea, let's get married!

AUDREY: You're funny.

TOUCHSTONE: I know. Listen, you're in the play because, well... they thought it would be ironic for me to fall in love.

AUDREY: Ah, you're so romantic, too. Ok. By the way, the name's Audrey.

TOUCHSTONE: Sweet! I'm Touchstone!

(they hold hands and exit)

ACT 4 SCENE 3

(enter ROSALIND [Ganymede] and CELIA [Aliena])

ROSALIND: He's late again, this time TWO hours! What a nincompoop! Why do I love him so?

(enter OLIVER)

OLIVER: I'm looking for a young guy and a... *(suddenly seeing CELIA's beauty)* BEAUTIFUL maiden... wow... Is this you?

CELIA: We are.

OLIVER: I bring a message from Orlando.

ROSALIND: This better be good.

OLIVER: Oh, it is! I was asleep in the forest when a green and gilded snake was about to attack me, and he saved me!

ROSALIND: That's it?

OLIVER: No! It gets better... THEN a lioness was lurking nearby about to eat me, and he fought the lioness to save me!

ROSALIND: Ok, that's better...

OLIVER: AND... he did this for me, HIS BROTHER, who kept trying to kill him! He's such a good person and I'm a dork! See... his blood!

(OLIVER hands bloody handkerchief to ROSALIND)

ROSALIND: Oh, Orlando! *(swoons)*

CELIA: How now, Ganymede!

OLIVER: Hmmm... I wonder why he did that? Hey, wake up... it's just blood. You lack a man's heart.

ROSALIND: Ahhh... I was acting the part of Rosalind for Orlando's sake... yeah!

OLIVER: Yeah, ok. I'll let him know that... *(aside)* strange.

(ALL exit)

ACT 5 SCENE 1

(enter OLIVER and ORLANDO)

OLIVER: Hey brother, I love Aliena and we are getting married!

ORLANDO: WHAT? You two literally met a minute ago.

OLIVER: Right?! I took one look at her and BAM, the shepherd's life for me!

ORLANDO: Ok, well, let your wedding be tomorrow.

OLIVER: Sweet! And I haven't seen her for like, 2 minutes, so... later!

(OLIVER exits; enter ROSALIND [Ganymede])

ORLANDO: *(to audience)* Oh look, here comes my "Rosalind".

ROSALIND: Hey, why do you look so sad.

ORLANDO: My brother's happiness tomorrow will match my sadness. I long for Rosalind.

ROSALIND: Okay, I've been keeping this a secret, but... I am a magician!

ORLANDO: I'm sorry, what?

ROSALIND: Listen, if you do love Rosalind, then tomorrow, at your brother's wedding, shall you marry her!

ORLANDO: How?!

ROSALIND: Easy, it's a Shakespeare comedy, and EVERYONE gets married at the end of those!

ORLANDO: Ohhhh...

(ALL exit)

ACT 5 SCENE 2

(enter TOUCHSTONE and AUDREY)

TOUCHSTONE: The fool doth think he is wise, but the wise man knows himself to be a fool.

AUDREY: You are so smart and funny!

TOUCHSTONE: I know.

AUDREY: Hey, everyone else is getting married tomorrow. Do you want to?

TOUCHSTONE: And you are brilliant! Yes!

AUDREY: SWEET!!!

(ALL exit)

ACT 5 SCENE 3

(enter DUKE SENIOR, OLIVER, ORLANDO, CELIA [Aliena], and ROSALIND [Ganymede])

DUKE S: *(to ORLANDO)* Do you believe the boy can do all that he hath promised?

ORLANDO: If it means I have to believe in magic, then yes!

ROSALIND: Ok, everyone, let's refresh! If I bring Rosalind, you'll marry her?

ORLANDO: Yep!

ROSALIND: Great! Give us a minute.

(exit ROSALIND and CELIA)

DUKE S: Have you noticed that Ganymede sure looks a lot like Rosalind?

OLIVER: Right? He's so lucky to find such a doppelganger!

(enter TOUCHSTONE and AUDREY)

TOUCHSTONE: Are we late?

DUKE S: Nope, the party's just getting started!

AUDREY: Sweet! *(pointing at herself)* Look how lucky he got!

(enter ROSALIND [Ganymede] and CELIA as herself)

ROSALIND: Look who I brought! *(presenting CELIA to OLIVER)*

OLIVER: *(noticing CELIA)* Wow! You clean up well!

CELIA: Yep!

ROSALIND: And I brought Rosalind! *(removes disguise)*

DUKE S: My daughter!

ORLANDO: My Rosalind!

ROSALIND: See, I told you. Magic! Oh, and more magic... we're all married now! Boom!

ALL: Yeah!

(ALL exit except ROSALIND)

EPILOGUE

ROSALIND: Ok, we're done here. Why don't you go grab your loved ones and party too! Bye!

THE END

NOTES

The 20-Minute or so
As You Like It

By William Shakespeare
Creatively modified by
Brendan P. Kelso

9 - 12 Actors

CAST OF CHARACTERS:

ROSALIND (later Ganymede): our heroine! And Duke Senior's daughter

CELIA (later Aliena): Rosalind's best friend; Duke Fredrick's daughter

TOUCHSTONE: a clown who is funny

[1]**DUKE FREDRICK:** rotten duke who took Duke Senior's throne

DUKE SENIOR: happily lives in the woods with his merry men

OLIVER: Orlando's terrible older brother

ORLANDO: Oliver's younger brother; LOVES Rosalind

[2]**CHARLES:** kingdom's wrestler (think WWE!)

[3]**JAQUES:** a melancholy man (with a FAMOUS speech)

[1]**SILVIUS:** a young shepherd who randomly walks around the forest; loves Phebe

[3]**PHEBE:** snobby girl who lives in the forest

[2]**AUDREY:** loves Touchstone

The same actors can play the following part:
[1]DUKE FREDRICK and SILVIUS
[2]AUDREY and CHARLES
[3]PHEBE and JAQUES

Located at the back of the book is a simple pronunciation key for the names and some words throughout the play.

ACT 1 SCENE 1
ORCHARD OF OLIVER'S HOUSE

(enter ORLANDO addressing audience)

ORLANDO: I am soooo bummed. Why, you ask? Well, Dad just died AND he left ALL his money to my older brother, Oliver. *(pauses and looks at audience member)* You don't get it, do you? Oliver DESPISES me and won't send me to school! I will no longer endure it! Here comes my snot-nosed brother now.

(enter OLIVER)

OLIVER: Well, if it's not my stinking little brother.

ORLANDO: I deserve my inheritance!

OLIVER: You deserve to live in the barn, Orlando!

ORLANDO: Aghhh! I've had it!!! *(they fight; ORLANDO is holding OLIVER)*

OLIVER: LET ME GO!!!

ORLANDO: Not until I get my money!

OLIVER: FINE!! *(ORLANDO lets go)* I pray you leave me. No one loves you anyway!!!

(ORLANDO exits; enter CHARLES)

OLIVER: Charles! How's life being the kingdom's wrestler?

CHARLES: Good. But, I have BIG news!

OLIVER: Yes? Do tell!

CHARLES: *(addressing audience and Oliver)* Well, Duke Fredrick just kicked his older brother, Duke Senior, out of the kingdom and usurped his throne!

OLIVER: You burped?

CHARLES: No! Usurped... he stole it!

OLIVER: Oh, fancy word. Go on.

CHARLES: So, Duke Senior now lives in the Forest of Arden with a band of merry men.

OLIVER: So... they live like Robin Hood?

CHARLES: Yes!

OLIVER: What about their daughters?

CHARLES: Rosalind, Duke Senior's daughter, is allowed to stay because she is best friends with Celia, Duke Fredrick's daughter.

OLIVER: Wow, nice exposition. It's almost as if you're setting the whole story up for the audience.

CHARLES: Exactly! But, I have a problem.

OLIVER: Really?

CHARLES: Yes. Your brother wants to fight me, the Great Charles, *(showing his muscles)* at the palace.

OLIVER: *(to audience)* Opportunity!

CHARLES: But, I'm gonna kick his butt, and it'll make me look bad... beating a nobleman.

OLIVER: *(with a bit of an evil snicker)* Oh, no, no, no, my friend! Orlando is cunning and deceitful and will use poison or entrap thee by some treacherous device. You need to crush him! No... SMASH him to pieces!

CHARLES: Smash?

OLIVER: Yes, smash, Charles. SMASH!

CHARLES: Charles, smash!!!

OLIVER: That's the spirit!

(ALL exit; CHARLES is repeating, "Charles, smash!")

ACT 1 SCENE 2
DUKE FREDRICK'S PALACE

(enter CELIA and ROSALIND)

CELIA: I pray thee, Rosalind, sweet my coz, be merry.

ROSALIND: If you can teach me how to forget a banished father, then I'll be merry.

CELIA: Tell ya what, when my father dies, I'll give you the kingdom back. Therefore, my dear Rose, be merry!

ROSALIND: Cool! I'm bored. I know! What think you of falling in love?

CELIA: Sounds like fun! *(enter TOUCHSTONE)* Well, hello clown, how are you today?

TOUCHSTONE: Joke: What was the nickname for the knight who ruled the fort? Fortnight!

ROSALIND: Ha ha! *(pauses)* I don't get it.

TOUCHSTONE: You know, fort-knight... aghh, nevermind. Here come the Duke and the wrestlers.

(enter DUKE FREDRICK, CHARLES, and ORLANDO)

DUKE F: How now, daughter and niece, here to see the wrestling?

CELIA: Yep!

ROSALIND: *(to ORLANDO)* Hey, that guy's pretty strong. Are you sure you want to get your butt kicked?

ORLANDO: *(warming up and not noticing ROSALIND)* Me? Hah! I will beat him with the strength of my youth! *(poses)*

CELIA: You know, this is the perfect time to panic and run.

ORLANDO: Bah! My brother detests me and I have little money, so I have nothing left to lose. Let's rumble!

DUKE F. *(addresses audience)* Ladies and gentlemen! In this corner, Charles the Magnificent! *(EVERYONE cheers)* and in this corner... *(to ORLANDO)* Uh... what's your name, kid?

ORLANDO: *(thinks)*... Captain O!

DUKE F. Captain O? K, he's going to get smashed!!! *(ROSALIND and CELIA cheer)*

CHARLES: Charles, SMASH!!!

ROSALIND: Now Hercules be thy speed, young man!

(they wrestle and ORLANDO wins)

DUKE F. What is thy name, young man?

ORLANDO: Orlando, my liege.

DUKE F. As in Sir Roland's son? My enemy? Humph!!! Now I'm mad! Let's leave.

(DUKE F exits)

ORLANDO: I am proud to be Sir Roland's son.

ROSALIND: My father loved Sir Roland.

ORLANDO: *(stunned by ROSALIND'S beauty)* Ahhh... wow... ohhh...

CELIA: *(pats ORLANDO on the back)* Well said, Captain O. Shall we go, coz?

ROSALIND: Hey, you're kinda cute.

ORLANDO: Ahhh...ohhh...

ROSALIND: Fare you well.

(CELIA and ROSALIND exit)

ORLANDO: *(to audience)* What passion hangs these weights upon my tongue? *(mocking himself)* Ahhhh... ohhhh... I'm such a fool! But, I gotta go! From tyrant duke unto a tyrant brother, how fun! But, heavenly Rosalind!

(ALL exit)

ACT 1 SCENE 3

DUKE FREDRICK'S PALACE

(enter CELIA and ROSALIND)

ROSALIND: Oh, Orlando!

CELIA: Cheer up, the play just started. I'm SURE we will see him again! But, here comes my dad with his eyes full of anger.

(enter DUKE FREDRICK)

DUKE F. *(to ROSALIND)* You! You're out of my kingdom! Okay, bye!

ROSALIND: Wait, what.. huh?! But why?

DUKE F. You like that Orlando guy and I trust thee not. Thou art thy father's daughter, there's enough.

CELIA: *(steps forward)* But daddy...

DUKE F. *(to CELIA)* STOP! Open not thy lips. She is banished.

(DUKE F exits)

CELIA: AHHHH!!! I'm soooo mad! *(screams offstage towards DUKE F)* Father, seek another heir! You banished her and hath banished me!

ROSALIND: Wow, that was dramatic. Where shall we go?

CELIA: The Forest of Arden to find your dad.

ROSALIND: The forest? We have to be careful, beauty provoketh thieves sooner than gold.

CELIA: Then, we'll disguise ourselves!

ROSALIND: Great idea! I'll dress as a man, as Jove's own page, Ganymede.

CELIA: And I'll be a poor shepherd girl.

ROSALIND: Why?

CELIA: Because I can! Now, to liberty, and not to banishment!

ROSALIND & CELIA: Yeah!

(ALL exit)

ACT 2 SCENES 1 & 2

THE FOREST AND THE PALACE

(enter DUKE SENIOR on one side of stage; enter DUKE FREDRICK on the other; they are in separate scenes but juxtaposed on stage; they address the audience)

DUKE S: I LOVE country life. Fresh air, beautiful trees, quiet streams, and peaceful animals.

DUKE F: I LOVE being the duke! Ruling everyone and my lords groveling to me. *(yelling offstage)* Speaking of which, where's my servant?! Someone grovel to me!!!

OFFSTAGE VOICE: You are most magnificent, your grace!

DUKE F: That's better!

DUKE S: You know, I do love teasing melancholy Jaques! He is always such a downer! Come! Let's have some fun!

(DUKE SENIOR exits; note flies onto stage)

DUKE F: *(picks up note)* Ah, must be more praise for the great me! *(reading)* Rosalind, your daughter, and the clown, have all left the kingdom to look for Duke Senior and to find Orlando. *(to audience)* WHAT the what!?!? I need to find Orlando's brother, Oliver! *(starts leaving)* NOW!!! *(offstage we hear, "yes sir!!!")*

(DUKE F exits)

ACT 2 SCENE 3

BEFORE OLIVER'S HOUSE

(enter ORLANDO addresses audience)

ORLANDO: So, rumor has it that my brother, Oliver, is planning on killing me. Well, I've got nothin' left here, so, I'm going to run off into the forest. Bye!

(ORLANDO exits)

ACT 2 SCENE 4

FOREST OF ARDEN

(enter ROSALIND [Ganymede], and CELIA [Aliena], and TOUCHSTONE)

ROSALIND: How weary are my spirits. Finally, we are here. This is the Forest of Arden.

TOUCHSTONE: I have no spirits, my legs hurt. *(lays down)*

CELIA: I cannot go any further. Touchstone, tell me a joke.

TOUCHSTONE: Knock, knock.

CELIA: Who's there?

TOUCHSTONE: No one! I'm too tired to answer! *(pretends to sleep)*

(enter SILVIUS wandering aimlessly, not seeing the others)

SILVIUS: *(dreamy)* Oh, I SOOOOOOO love Phebe!!! *(to audience)* Hi. Have you seen Phebe? Wow... She's so... yeah... *(drifts off)* I'm going to continue wandering aimlessly through the woods thinking of my dear Phebe. O Phebe, Phebe, Phebe!

(SILVIUS wanders offstage)

ROSALIND: *(mocking him)* O Phebe, Phebe, Phebe... Hmmm... This place is getting interesting.

CELIA: What are you thinking about?

ROSALIND: Having more fun.

CELIA: Great! Let's go!

(ALL exit)

THE FOREST

(enter JAQUES; offstage someone is singing some simple country song)

JAQUES: *(yelling)* Quit singing that dreadful song! *(to audience)* Oh, hello. Question. WHO, in their right mind, would leave riches to move to the woods. *(yelling offstage)* You're all demented! *(to audience)* I'm randomly walking off in search of nothing. See ya!

(JAQUES exits; enter DUKE SENIOR)

DUKE S: *(to audience)* Have you seen Jaques? *(pauses as he seems to interact with audience to find JAQUES)* No? Yes? That way? Thanks! *(enter JAQUES)* Ah, Jaques. I was just looking for you.

JAQUES: *(very happy)* HELLO!

DUKE S: What, you look merrily! Very unlike you.

JAQUES: A fool, a fool! I met a fool i' the forest. I WANT to be a fool! I found my life's calling!

DUKE S: You do realize we already think you're a fool? Plus, the play already has a fool, so...

JAQUES: Whatever.

(ORLANDO enters brandishing sword)

ORLANDO: Forbear and eat no more, or I will have to kill you all! In other words, gimmie food or die!

DUKE S: Food? Is that all? Well then, come and join us.

ORLANDO: Really? Cool.

JAQUES: *(addresses everyone)* Did you know...

All the world's a stage,

And all the men and women merely players:

They have their exits and their entrances;

And one man in his time plays many parts,

His acts being seven ages. At first the infant,

Mewling and puking...

ORLANDO: Gross! We're eating here!

DUKE S: There goes my appetite... *(looking at ORLANDO)* Hey, aren't you the good Sir Roland's son, my old friend?

ORLANDO: Yes.

DUKE S: Well, welcome to the tribe!

(ALL exit)

ACT 3 SCENE 1

A ROOM IN THE PALACE

(enter DUKE F and OLIVER)

DUKE F: You!

OLIVER: Yes, sir!

DUKE F: I need you to find and kill your brother, or I kill you, capisce? *(pronounced Kuh-PEESH)*

OLIVER: Of course! I never loved my brother in my life.

DUKE F: Good! Now get out of here! *(OLIVER runs off; to audience)* Wow, I love being powerful!!!

(DUKE F exits)

ACT 3 SCENE 2

THE FOREST

(for the rest of the play)

(enter ORLANDO, leaving poems lying around; addresses audience)

ORLANDO: Oh, my heart!!! My achy-breaky heart! I LOVE Rosalind sooooo much that I'm leaving random poems scattered throughout the forest. Here, have some... go on, read it to all... *(audience member reads, it's TERRIBLE)* Oh... isn't it WONDERFUL?! *(exits dancing happily)*

(enter ROSALIND [Ganymede], CELIA [Aliena], and TOUCHSTONE)

ROSALIND: *(picks up a poem)* What's this? *(reads)* "From the east to the western Ind; No jewel is like Rosalind." Ahhh, how cute.

TOUCHSTONE: Oh, garbage I say... *(in a mocking voice)*

Oh, I'm a fool!

Look at me drool,

Over some girl,

BLEH! Makes me want to hurl!

CELIA: Oh quiet, Touchstone! You'll find love to be awesome one day, too!

TOUCHSTONE: Never! *(exits)*

CELIA: I think I know who wrote these. *(reads another aloud)* "Rosalind is beautiful, and my love is suitable... for her." Wow, these are terrible...

ROSALIND: True. Wait, what?! You know... WHO?!!!

CELIA: Well, I'm not sure...

ROSALIND: But who is it?!!! *(rambles)* What does he look like? Will I like him? Is he ugly?

CELIA: Well...

ROSALIND: *(continuing right over CELIA)* What if he's short? Or he doesn't shower? Or has a mustache? Ewww... Wait... What if he's THE ONE?

CELIA: Well, this IS a romantic comedy...

ROSALIND: *(continuing to ramble)* Can I get my father to approve? Why is this confusing? Are you pulling my leg? Is that gas I'm feeling? Who gave me coffee? Did you write these?

CELIA: What? Yes. No. STOP! No... aghhh... you ask too many questions!

ROSALIND: Do you not know I am a woman? When I think, I must speak!

CELIA: Sheesh! It is young Orlando, that doofus wrestling guy we met.

ROSALIND: Oh... *(suddenly realizing)* OHHHH... HIM.... Oh, he's dreamy...

CELIA: Yes "him"... and look, here "him" is now...

(enter ORLANDO and JAQUES, laughing)

ORLANDO: No, you're Monsieur Melancholy.

JAQUES: Stop it, Signior Love.

ORLANDO: Am not! Ok, I am...

(JAQUES exits)

ROSALIND: You are what?

ORLANDO: In love... wait, who are you?

ROSALIND: The name is Ganymede.

ORLANDO: Gany-who?

ROSALIND: Nevermind. *(to CELIA)* I'm going to speak to him like a saucy lackey and play the knave with him.

CELIA: What, was that even English?

ROSALIND: It means, I'm going to mess with him.

CELIA: Oh!

ROSALIND: *(to ORLANDO)* We were laughing at some lovesick lunatic who was going around carving the name, "Rosalind" on all the trees.

ORLANDO: That be me that is so love-shaked! Do you have a remedy for this feeling?

ROSALIND: I can cure you of this lovesickness.

ORLANDO: Really? How?

ROSALIND: I will pretend I'm this... uh... this Rosalind and you will come every day and woo me.

ORLANDO: What? You're a dude, and you look NOTHING like my fair Rosalind.

ROSALIND: Nothing? Really? Are you sure? Maybe the lighting is off... anyway, pretend, and I will cure you of your lovesick lunacy!

ORLANDO: This is confusing.

ROSALIND: This is Shakespeare, just do it.

ORLANDO: With all my heart, good youth, I'll do as you say.

ROSALIND: And don't call me 'good youth', call me Rosalind!

ORLANDO: As you like it! *(to audience)* Get it?

(ALL exit)

ACT 3 SCENE 3

(enter ROSALIND [Ganymede], SILVIUS, and PHEBE; ROSALIND watching)

SILVIUS: Sweet Phebe, do not scorn me, say you love me!

PHEBE: Eew! No way. You're gross and smell bad.

SILVIUS: I swear I'll shower once a week if you'll love me!

PHEBE: No! Come not thou near me.

ROSALIND: *(interrupting)* Hello! *(to PHEBE)* Listen, this guy's totally into you, and you're being a pain.

PHEBE: But...

ROSALIND: Ah, ahh... just hush... *(looks her over)* They're not too many guys in this forest, and you should sell when you can, you are not for all markets.

SILVIUS: You sound smart! Who are you?

ROSALIND: Call me the Love Doctor!

PHEBE: Of course... cause I'm TOTALLY in love with YOU!!!

ROSALIND: Whaaaat? No.. no... no! Just fall in love with him and let's keep this play going! *(ROSALIND exits)*

PHEBE: Who was that peevish boy who was SO cute!

SILVIUS: Dunno. But hey, I still like you.

PHEBE: Well, since you're the only one left on stage, fine, I'll hang out with you for the rest of the show.

SILVIUS: I'm good with that!

(ALL exit)

ACT 4 SCENE 1

(enter ROSALIND [Ganymede] and CELIA [Aliena]; pause then enter ORLANDO)

ORLANDO: Good day, dear Rosalind.

ROSALIND: Don't 'good day' me! You're late!

ORLANDO: I'm only an hour late.

ROSALIND: Break an hour's promise in love? Then you don't love at all!

ORLANDO: But...

ROSALIND: Get out of here and try this again! *(ORLANDO waits, confused)* Go!

(ORLANDO exits then re-enters)

ORLANDO: Ok, I'm back!

ROSALIND: That's not how you greet a love! Go! Do it again! If you want Rosalind to love you, then you need to WOOOO her! Now go! Come back a better woo-er!

(CELIA shoves ORLANDO off stage; ORLANDO re-enters)

ORLANDO: My dear, Rosalind...

ROSALIND: *(interrupting)* Better... Now, come, woo me, woo me.

ORLANDO: Ok... I love you.

ROSALIND: *(mocking ORLANDO)* I love you... blah, blah, blah... you do not love. Show me LOVE!

ORLANDO: I die for love and I would die for you!

ROSALIND: Better. But, you saw what happened to Romeo & Juliet, dying for love may not be the best thing. I got it! Aliena, act as a priest and marry us!

CELIA: *(shocked)* What?!

ROSALIND: Priest, you know... marriage! Just do it!

CELIA: Okey-dokey. *(they hold hands)* Will you, Orlando, have to wife this Rosalind?

ORLANDO: I will. I take thee, Rosalind, for a wife.

ROSALIND: *(feeling love-struck)* Wow. Ok, you're doing great!

ORLANDO: But, will my Rosalind do so?

ROSALIND: By my life, she will do as I do! *(to audience)* Really, she will!

ORLANDO: O, but she is wise!

ROSALIND: *(to audience)* Very true! *(to ORLANDO)* Now, get out of here and don't be late again!

ORLANDO: Aye, sweet Rosalind. Adieu! *(exits)*

CELIA: Wow, you really got him in shape!

ROSALIND: *(sighs heavily)* I know...

CELIA: *(pulling ROSALIND offstage)* Come on crazy Cupid.

(ALL exit)

ACT 4 SCENE 2

(enter AUDREY and TOUCHSTONE)

TOUCHSTONE: Hey, you're cute.

AUDREY: Ahhh... thanks!

TOUCHSTONE: I have an idea, let's get married!

AUDREY: You're funny.

TOUCHSTONE: I know. Listen, you're in the play because, well... they thought it would be ironic for me to fall in love.

AUDREY: Ah, you're so romantic, too. Ok. By the way, the name's Audrey.

TOUCHSTONE: Sweet! I'm Touchstone!

(they hold hands and exit)

ACT 4 SCENE 3

(enter ROSALIND [Ganymede] and CELIA [Aliena])

ROSALIND: He's late again, this time TWO hours! What a nincompoop! Why do I love him so?

CELIA: You're putting too much pressure on him. Look who comes here.

(enter SILVIUS)

SILVIUS: Ganymede, Phebe wrote this letter for me to give to you.

ROSALIND: *(reading letter)* Wow, she's rude.

SILVIUS: But, I love her.

ROSALIND: You are a fool.

SILVIUS: True. But I still love her.

ROSALIND: Listen, it says she likes Ganymede.

SILVIUS: Isn't that you?

ROSALIND: Ahhh, yeah. I mean she likes me. So, tell her that if she loves me, that I will never love her unless she loves you.

SILVIUS: Huh?

ROSALIND: Exactly! Now go!

(CELIA shoves SILVIUS off stage who is very confused)

CELIA: Alas, poor shepherd.

(enter OLIVER)

OLIVER: I'm looking for a young guy and a... *(suddenly seeing CELIA's beauty)* BEAUTIFUL maiden... wow... Is this you?

CELIA: We are.

OLIVER: I bring a message from Orlando.

ROSALIND: This better be good.

OLIVER: Oh, it is! I was asleep in the forest when a green and gilded snake was about to attack me, and he saved me!

ROSALIND: That's it?

OLIVER: No! It gets better... THEN a lioness was lurking nearby about to eat me, and he fought the lioness to save me!

ROSALIND: Ok, that's better...

OLIVER: AND... he did this for me, HIS BROTHER, who kept trying to kill him! He's such a good person and I'm a dork! See... his blood!

(OLIVER hands bloody handkerchief to ROSALIND)

ROSALIND: Oh, Orlando! *(swoons)*

CELIA: How now, Ganymede!

OLIVER: Hmmm... I wonder why he did that? Hey, wake up... it's just blood. You lack a man's heart.

ROSALIND: Ahhh... I was acting the part of Rosalind for Orlando's sake... yeah!

OLIVER: Yeah, ok. I'll let him know that... *(aside)* strange.

(ALL exit)

ACT 5 SCENE 1

(enter OLIVER and ORLANDO)

OLIVER: Hey brother, I love Aliena and we are getting married!

ORLANDO: WHAT? You two literally met a minute ago.

OLIVER: Right?! I took one look at her and BAM, the shepherd's life for me!

ORLANDO: Ok, well, let your wedding be tomorrow.

OLIVER: Sweet! And I haven't seen her for like, 2 minutes, so... later!

(OLIVER exits; enter ROSALIND [Ganymede])

ORLANDO: *(to audience)* Oh look, here comes my "Rosalind".

ROSALIND: Hey, why do you look so sad.

ORLANDO: My brother's happiness tomorrow will match my sadness. I long for Rosalind.

ROSALIND: Okay, I've been keeping this a secret, but... I am a magician!

ORLANDO: I'm sorry, what?

ROSALIND: Listen, if you do love Rosalind, then tomorrow, at your brother's wedding, shall you marry her!

ORLANDO: How?!

(enter PHEBE and SILVIUS)

PHEBE: *(to ROSALIND)* Ganymede, I love you.

SILVIUS: Phebe, I love you.

ORLANDO: *(to no one)* Rosalind, I love you.

ROSALIND: Who do you speak to?

ORLANDO: To her that is not here.

ROSALIND: Ok, you love fools, all of you meet here tomorrow and I promise you, you will marry the one you love!

PHEBE: Wait, how do you know this?

ROSALIND: Easy, it's a Shakespeare comedy, and EVERYONE gets married at the end of those!

ALL: Ohhhh...

(ALL exit)

ACT 5 SCENE 2

(enter TOUCHSTONE and AUDREY)

TOUCHSTONE: The fool doth think he is wise, but the wise man knows himself to be a fool.

AUDREY: You are so smart and funny!

TOUCHSTONE: I know.

AUDREY: Hey, everyone else is getting married tomorrow. Do you want to?

TOUCHSTONE: And you are brilliant! Yes!

AUDREY: SWEET!!!

(ALL exit)

ACT 5 SCENE 3

(enter DUKE SENIOR, OLIVER, ORLANDO, SILVIUS, PHEBE, CELIA [Aliena], and ROSALIND [Ganymede])

DUKE S: *(to ORLANDO)* Do you believe the boy can do all that he hath promised?

ORLANDO: If it means I have to believe in magic, then yes!

ROSALIND: Ok, everyone, let's refresh! If I bring Rosalind, you'll marry her?

ORLANDO: Yep!

ROSALIND: And you'll marry me, if I be willing? But, if you do refuse, you'll marry this most faithful shepherd?

PHEBE: Refuse you? Suuure... I'll marry anyone you want me to! I'll even marry that random audience member right there!

ROSALIND: Good. And you're good with this, right?

SILVIUS: Oh, yeah!

ROSALIND: Great! Give us a minute.

(exit ROSALIND and CELIA)

DUKE S: Have you noticed that Ganymede sure looks a lot like Rosalind?

OLIVER: Right? He's so lucky to find such a doppelganger!

(enter TOUCHSTONE and AUDREY)

TOUCHSTONE: Are we late?

DUKE S: Nope, the party's just getting started!

AUDREY: Sweet! *(pointing at herself)* Look how lucky he got!

(enter ROSALIND [Ganymede] and CELIA as herself)

ROSALIND: Look who I brought! *(presenting CELIA to OLIVER)*

OLIVER: *(noticing CELIA)* Wow! You clean up well!

CELIA: Yep!

ROSALIND: And I brought Rosalind! *(removes disguise)*

DUKE S: My daughter!

ORLANDO: My Rosalind!

PHEBE: My gosh, I have to marry the shepherd now?!

SILVIUS: Yes!

ROSALIND: See, I told you. Magic!

PHEBE: Ugh. Fine!

ROSALIND: Oh, and more magic... we're all married now! Boom!

ALL: Yeah!

(ALL exit except ROSALIND)

EPILOGUE

ROSALIND: Ok, we're done here. Why don't you go grab your loved ones and party too! Bye!

THE END

The 25-Minute or so
As You Like It
By William Shakespeare
Creatively modified by
Brendan P. Kelso
12 - 17+ Actors

CAST OF CHARACTERS:

ROSALIND (later Ganymede): our heroine! And Duke Senior's daughter

CELIA (later Aliena): Rosalind's best friend; Duke Fredrick's daughter

TOUCHSTONE: a clown who is funny

[2]DUKE FREDRICK: rotten duke who took Duke Senior's throne

DUKE SENIOR: happily lives in the woods with his merry men

[5]OLIVER: Orlando's terrible older brother

ORLANDO: Oliver's younger brother; LOVES Rosalind

[1]ADAM: Orlando's faithful servant

[4]CHARLES: kingdom's wrestler (think WWE!)

JAQUES: a melancholy man (with a FAMOUS speech)

HYMEN: God of marriage (yes, an actual god!)

[2]SILVIUS: a young shepherd who randomly walks around the forest; loves Phebe

[1]CORIN: another random shepherd

[3]PHEBE: snobby girl who lives in the forest

[4]AUDREY: loves Touchstone

[5]LORD AMIENS: Duke Senior's courtier

[3]DOTING LORD: Duke Fredrick's groveling lord

The same actors can play the following part:
[1]ADAM and CORIN same actor
[2]DUKE FREDRICK and SILVIUS
[3]PHEBE and DOTING LORD
[4]AUDREY and CHARLES
[5]LORD AMIENS and OLIVER

Extra actors can be doting Lords for Duke Frederick or other wrestlers.

Located at the back of the book is a simple pronunciation key for the names and some words throughout the play.

ACT 1 SCENE 1
ORCHARD OF OLIVER'S HOUSE

(enter ORLANDO and ADAM)

ORLANDO: Adam, I am sooo bummed.

ADAM: Why, Orlando?

ORLANDO: My dear servant, dad just died, BUT, that's not the worst. No. He left ALL his money to my older brother, Oliver.

ADAM: And that is bad because...

ORLANDO: Because Oliver DESPISES me and won't send me to school!

ADAM: Wow, that stinks. Oh look, yonder comes your brother, Oliver.

ORLANDO: I will no longer endure it!

(enter OLIVER)

OLIVER: Well, if it's not my stinking little brother.

ORLANDO: I deserve my inheritance!

OLIVER: You deserve to live in the barn, Orlando!

ORLANDO: Aghhh! I've had it!!! *(they start to fight; ORLANDO is holding OLIVER)*

OLIVER: LET ME GO!!!

ORLANDO: Not until I get my money!

OLIVER: FINE!! *(ORLANDO lets go)* I pray you leave me. No one loves you anyway!!! *(to ADAM)* And get you with him, you old dog.

(ORLANDO and ADAM exit; enter CHARLES)

OLIVER: Charles! How's life being the kingdom's wrestler?

CHARLES: Good. But, I have BIG news!

OLIVER: Yes? Do tell!

CHARLES: *(addressing audience and Oliver)* Well, Duke Fredrick just kicked his older brother, Duke Senior, out of the kingdom and usurped his throne!

OLIVER: You burped?

CHARLES: No! Usurped... he stole it!

OLIVER: Oh, fancy word. Go on.

CHARLES: So, Duke Senior now lives in the Forest of Arden with a band of merry men.

OLIVER: So... they live like Robin Hood?

CHARLES: Yes!

OLIVER: What about their daughters?

CHARLES: Rosalind, Duke Senior's daughter, is allowed to stay because she is best friends with Celia, Duke Fredrick's daughter.

OLIVER: Wow, nice exposition. It's almost as if you're setting the whole story up for the audience.

CHARLES: Exactly! But, I have a problem.

OLIVER: Really?

CHARLES: Yes. Your brother wants to fight me, the Great Charles, *(showing his muscles)* at the palace.

OLIVER: *(to audience)* Opportunity!

CHARLES: But, I'm gonna kick his butt, and it'll make me look bad... beating a nobleman.

OLIVER: *(with a bit of an evil snicker)* Oh, no, no, no, my friend! Orlando is cunning and deceitful and will use poison or entrap thee by some treacherous device. You need to crush him! No... SMASH him to pieces!

CHARLES: Smash?

OLIVER: Yes, smash, Charles. SMASH!

CHARLES: Charles, smash!!!

OLIVER: That's the spirit!

(ALL exit; CHARLES is repeating, "Charles, smash!")

DUKE FREDRICK'S PALACE

(enter CELIA and ROSALIND)

CELIA: I pray thee, Rosalind, sweet my coz, be merry.

ROSALIND: If you can teach me how to forget a banished father, then I'll be merry.

CELIA: Tell ya what, when my father dies, I'll give you the kingdom back. Therefore, my dear Rose, be merry!

ROSALIND: Cool! I'm bored. I know! What think you of falling in love?

CELIA: Sounds like fun! *(enter TOUCHSTONE)* Well, hello clown, how are you today?

TOUCHSTONE: Joke: What was the nickname for the knight who ruled the fort? Fortnight!

ROSALIND: Ha ha! *(pauses)* I don't get it.

TOUCHSTONE: You know, fort-knight... aghh, nevermind. Here come the Duke and the wrestlers.

(enter DUKE FREDRICK, CHARLES, ORLANDO, and DOTING LORD saying random wonderful things about the duke)

DUKE F: How now, daughter and niece, here to see the wrestling?

CELIA: Yep!

ROSALIND: *(to ORLANDO)* Hey, that guy's pretty strong. Are you sure you want to get your butt kicked?

ORLANDO: *(warming up and not noticing ROSALIND)* Me? Hah! I will beat him with the strength of my youth! *(poses)*

CELIA: You know, this is the perfect time to panic and run.

ORLANDO: Bah! My brother detests me and I have little money, so I have nothing left to lose. Let's rumble!

DUKE F: *(addresses audience)* Ladies and gentlemen! In this corner, Charles the Magnificent! *(EVERYONE cheers)* and in this corner... *(to ORLANDO)* Uh... what's your name, kid?

ORLANDO: *(thinks)*... Captain O!

DUKE F: Captain O? K, he's going to get smashed!!! *(ROSALIND and CELIA cheer)*

CHARLES: Charles, SMASH!!!

ROSALIND: Now Hercules be thy speed, young man!

(they wrestle and ORLANDO wins)

DUKE F: What is thy name, young man?

ORLANDO: Orlando, my liege.

DUKE F: As in Sir Roland's son? My enemy? Humph!!! Now I'm mad! Let's leave.

(DUKE F and DOTING LORD exit)

ORLANDO: I am proud to be Sir Roland's son.

ROSALIND: My father loved Sir Roland.

ORLANDO: *(stunned by ROSALIND'S beauty)* Ahhh... wow... ohhh...

CELIA: *(pats ORLANDO on the back)* Well said, Captain O. Shall we go, coz?

ROSALIND: Hey, you're kinda cute.

ORLANDO: Ahhh...ohhh...

ROSALIND: Fare you well.

(CELIA and ROSALIND exit)

ORLANDO: *(to audience)* What passion hangs these weights upon my tongue? *(mocking himself)* Ahhh... ohhh... I'm such a fool! But, I gotta go! From tyrant duke unto a tyrant brother, how fun! But, heavenly Rosalind!

(ALL exit)

ACT 1 SCENE 3

DUKE FREDRICK'S PALACE

(enter CELIA and ROSALIND)

ROSALIND: Oh, Orlando!

CELIA: Cheer up, the play just started. I'm SURE we will see him again! But, here comes my dad with his eyes full of anger.

(enter DUKE FREDRICK with DOTING LORD saying random wonderful things)

DUKE F. *(to ROSALIND)* You! You're out of my kingdom! Okay, bye!

ROSALIND: Wait, what.. huh?! But why?

DUKE F. You like that Orlando guy and I trust thee not. Thou art thy father's daughter, there's enough.

CELIA: *(steps forward)* But daddy...

DUKE F. *(to CELIA)* STOP! Open not thy lips. She is banished.

(DUKE F and LORD exit doting about the duke)

CELIA: AHHHH!!! I'm soooo mad! *(screams offstage towards DUKE F)* Father, seek another heir! You banished her and hath banished me!

ROSALIND: Wow, that was dramatic. Where shall we go?

CELIA: The Forest of Arden to find your dad.

ROSALIND: The forest? We have to be careful, beauty provoketh thieves sooner than gold.

CELIA: Then, we'll disguise ourselves!

ROSALIND: Great idea! I'll dress as a man, as Jove's own page, Ganymede.

CELIA: And I'll be a poor shepherd girl.

ROSALIND: Why?

CELIA: Because I can! Now, to liberty, and not to banishment!

ROSALIND & CELIA: Yeah!

(ALL exit)

ACT 2 SCENES 1 & 2

THE FOREST AND THE PALACE

(enter DUKE SENIOR and AMIENS on one side of stage; enter DUKE FREDRICK and DOTING LORD on the other; they are in separate scenes but juxtaposed on stage)

DUKE S: I LOVE country life. Fresh air, beautiful trees, quiet streams, and peaceful animals.

DUKE F: I LOVE being the duke! Ruling everyone and my lords groveling to me. *(to his LORD)* Tie my shoes.

DOTING LORD: With pleasure, your grace!

AMIENS: Yes, all good things are wild and free.

DOTING LORD: My duke, you are most magnificent.

AMIENS: Sir, I hear that Jaques is nearby, should we go have some fun with him?

DUKE S: Oh yes! I do love teasing melancholy Jaques! He is always such a downer!

(DUKE SENIOR and AMIENS exit)

DOTING LORD: Sir, I hear Rosalind, your daughter, and the clown, have all left the kingdom to look for Duke Senior. You know, the guy whose crown you stole.

DUKE F: WHAT!?!?

DOTING LORD: And rumor has it, to find Orlando, too!

DUKE F: WHAT THE WHAT!?!? Go get me his brother, Oliver! *(slight pause)* NOW!!!

(LORD runs off scared; ALL exit)

ACT 2 SCENE 3

BEFORE OLIVER'S HOUSE

(enter ORLANDO and ADAM)

ADAM: My young master, what are you doing here?

ORLANDO: Um, I live here?

ADAM: Yeah... not anymore. Your brother, Oliver, is planning on burning down the house... tonight... WITH YOU IN IT!

ORLANDO: Oh. *(doesn't move)*

ADAM: MOVE! Master, go on!

ORLANDO: Right! Let's run off into the forest!

ADAM: Sounds like a well thought out plan!

(ALL exit)

ACT 2 SCENE 4

FOREST OF ARDEN

(enter ROSALIND [Ganymede], and CELIA [Aliena], and TOUCHSTONE)

ROSALIND: How weary are my spirits. Finally, we are here. This is the Forest of Arden.

TOUCHSTONE: I have no spirits, my legs hurt. *(lays down)*

CELIA: I cannot go any further. Touchstone, tell me a joke.

TOUCHSTONE: Knock, knock.

CELIA: Who's there?

TOUCHSTONE: No one! I'm too tired to answer! *(pretends to sleep)*

(enter SILVIUS and CORIN, not seeing the others)

SILVIUS: Oh, I SOOOOOOO love Phebe!!!

CORIN: Yes, Silvius, I know... Phebe this and Phebe that!!! And a thousand more times that I have forgotten!

SILVIUS: You're just jealous, Corin!

CORIN: Yeeeaaah, that's it. *(to audience)* And here I had it confused with annoying.

SILVIUS: Let's continue wandering aimlessly through the woods thinking of my dear Phebe. O Phebe, Phebe, Phebe!

(SILVIUS wanders offstage)

CORIN: *(mocking him)* O Phebe, Phebe, Phebe... bleh...

ROSALIND: Excuse me.

CORIN: Hello, sir. Where did you come from?

ROSALIND: Just hiding behind this tree over here. Do you know where we can get some shelter?

CORIN: I have a place nearby that's for sale.

CELIA: Great!

ROSALIND: Will buy it!

CORIN: Wow, that was fast.

ROSALIND: It's a short play, gotta keep it snappy! *(gives CORIN money)*

CORIN: Well then, go with me!

(ALL exit)

ACT 2 SCENES 5-7

THE FOREST

(enter AMIENS and JAQUES; AMIENS is singing some type of simple country song)

JAQUES: Quit singing that dreadful song!

AMIENS: But, it's so peaceful out here in the woods away from city life.

JAQUES: WHO, in their right mind, would leave riches to move to the woods. You're all demented! I'm randomly walking off in search of nothing. See ya!

(JAQUES exits; AMIENS shrugs and continues singing his song as he exits; enter ORLANDO and ADAM)

ADAM: O, I die for food! *(lies down on side of stage)* Measure out my grave. Farewell!

ORLANDO: Oh, quit being overly dramatic, you're not going to die, this isn't a tragedy. I'll get some food! You stay right... *(noticing ADAM is already asleep)* ... there.

(ORLANDO exits; enter DUKE SENIOR and AMIENS)

DUKE S: Where is Jaques?

AMIENS: I left him randomly wandering in the woods as he complained about life... AGAIN.

(enter JAQUES)

JAQUES: *(very happy)* HELLO!

DUKE S: What, you look merrily! Very unlike you.

JAQUES: A fool, a fool! I met a fool i' the forest. I WANT to be a fool! I found my life's calling!

DUKE S: You do realize we already think you're a fool? Plus, the play already has a fool, so...

JAQUES: Whatever.

(ORLANDO enters brandishing sword)

ORLANDO: Forbear and eat no more, or I will have to kill you all! In other words, gimmie food or die!

DUKE S: Food? Is that all? Well then, come and join us.

ORLANDO: Really? Cool. Hey Adam... food.

(ADAM wakes up and sits with the group)

ADAM: Sweet!

JAQUES: *(addresses everyone)* Did you know...

All the world's a stage,

And all the men and women merely players:

They have their exits and their entrances;

And one man in his time plays many parts,

His acts being seven ages. At first the infant,

Mewling and puking...

AMIENS: Gross! We're eating here!

DUKE S: There goes my appetite... *(looking at ORLANDO)* Hey, aren't you the good Sir Roland's son, my old friend?

ORLANDO: Yes.

DUKE S: Well, welcome to the tribe!

(ALL exit)

ACT 3 SCENE 1

A ROOM IN THE PALACE

(enter DUKE F, DOTING LORD, and OLIVER)

DUKE F: You!

OLIVER: Yes, sir!

DUKE F: I need you to find and kill your brother, or I kill you, capisce? *(pronounced Kuh-PEESH)*

OLIVER: Of course! I never loved my brother in my life.

DUKE F: Good! Now get out of here! *(to DOTING LORD)* Say more great things about me.

(ALL exit while LORD is saying amazing things about DUKE F)

ACT 3 SCENE 2

THE FOREST

(for the rest of the play)

(enter ORLANDO, leaving poems lying around; addresses audience)

ORLANDO: Oh, my heart!!! My achy-breaky heart! I LOVE Rosalind sooooo much that I'm leaving random poems scattered throughout the forest. Here, have some... go on, read it to all... *(audience member reads, it's TERRIBLE)* Oh... isn't it WONDERFUL?! *(exits dancing happily)*

(enter ROSALIND [Ganymede], CELIA [Aliena], and TOUCHSTONE)

ROSALIND: *(picks up a poem)* What's this? *(reads)* "From the east to the western Ind; No jewel is like Rosalind." Ahhh, how cute.

TOUCHSTONE: Oh, garbage I say... *(in a mocking voice)*

Oh, I'm a fool!

Look at me drool,

Over some girl,

BLEH! Makes me want to hurl!

CELIA: Oh quiet, Touchstone! You'll find love to be awesome one day, too!

TOUCHSTONE: Never! *(exits)*

CELIA: I think I know who wrote these. *(reads another aloud)* "Rosalind is beautiful, and my love is suitable... for her." Wow, these are terrible...

ROSALIND: True. Wait, what?! You know... WHO?!!!

CELIA: Well, I'm not sure...

ROSALIND: But who is it?!!! *(rambles)* What does he look like? Will I like him? Is he ugly?

CELIA: Well...

ROSALIND: *(continuing right over CELIA)* What if he's short? Or he doesn't shower? Or has a mustache? Ewww... Wait... What if he's THE ONE?

CELIA: Well, this IS a romantic comedy...

ROSALIND: *(continuing to ramble)* Can I get my father to approve? Why is this confusing? Are you pulling my leg? Is that gas I'm feeling? Who gave me coffee? Did you write these?

CELIA: What? Yes. No. STOP! No... aghhh... you ask too many questions!

ROSALIND: Do you not know I am a woman? When I think, I must speak!

CELIA: Sheesh! It is young Orlando, that doofus wrestling guy we met.

ROSALIND: Oh... *(suddenly realizing)* OHHHH... HIM.... Oh, he's dreamy...

CELIA: Yes "him"... and look, here "him" is now...

(enter ORLANDO and JAQUES, laughing)

ORLANDO: No, you're Monsieur Melancholy.

JAQUES: Stop it, Signior Love.

ORLANDO: Am not! Ok, I am...

(JAQUES exits)

ROSALIND: You are what?

ORLANDO: In love... wait, who are you?

ROSALIND: The name is Ganymede.

ORLANDO: Gany-who?

ROSALIND: Nevermind. *(to CELIA)* I'm going to speak to him like a saucy lackey and play the knave with him.

CELIA: What, was that even English?

ROSALIND: It means, I'm going to mess with him.

CELIA: Oh!

ROSALIND: *(to ORLANDO)* We were laughing at some lovesick lunatic who was going around carving the name, "Rosalind" on all the trees.

ORLANDO: That be me that is so love-shaked! Do you have a remedy for this feeling?

ROSALIND: I can cure you of this lovesickness.

ORLANDO: Really? How?

ROSALIND: I will pretend I'm this... uh... this Rosalind and you will come every day and woo me.

ORLANDO: What? You're a dude, and you look NOTHING like my fair Rosalind.

ROSALIND: Nothing? Really? Are you sure? Maybe the lighting is off... anyway, pretend, and I will cure you of your lovesick lunacy!

ORLANDO: This is confusing.

ROSALIND: This is Shakespeare, just do it.

ORLANDO: With all my heart, good youth, I'll do as you say.

ROSALIND: And don't call me 'good youth', call me Rosalind!

ORLANDO: As you like it! *(to audience)* Get it?

(ALL exit)

ACT 3 SCENE 3

(enter ROSALIND [Ganymede], SILVIUS, and PHEBE; ROSALIND watching)

SILVIUS: Sweet Phebe, do not scorn me, say you love me!

PHEBE: Eew! No way. You're gross and smell bad.

SILVIUS: I swear I'll shower once a week if you'll love me!

PHEBE: No! Come not thou near me.

ROSALIND: *(interrupting)* Hello! *(to PHEBE)* Listen, this guy's totally into you, and you're being a pain.

PHEBE: But...

ROSALIND: Ah, ahh... just hush... *(looks her over)* They're not too many guys in this forest, and you should sell when you can, you are not for all markets.

SILVIUS: You sound smart! Who are you?

ROSALIND: Call me the Love Doctor!

PHEBE: Of course... cause I'm TOTALLY in love with YOU!!!

ROSALIND: Whaaaaat? No.. no... no! Just fall in love with him and let's keep this play going! *(ROSALIND exits)*

PHEBE: Who was that peevish boy who was SO cute!

SILVIUS: Dunno. But hey, I still like you.

PHEBE: Well, since you're the only one left on stage, fine, I'll hang out with you for the rest of the show.

SILVIUS: I'm good with that!

(ALL exit)

ACT 4 SCENE 1

(enter ROSALIND [Ganymede] and CELIA [Aliena]; pause then enter ORLANDO)

ORLANDO: Good day, dear Rosalind.

ROSALIND: Don't 'good day' me! You're late!

ORLANDO: I'm only an hour late.

ROSALIND: Break an hour's promise in love? Then you don't love at all!

ORLANDO: But...

ROSALIND: Get out of here and try this again! *(ORLANDO waits, confused)* Go!

(ORLANDO exits then re-enters)

ORLANDO: Ok, I'm back!

ROSALIND: That's not how you greet a love! Go! Do it again! If you want Rosalind to love you, then you need to WOOOO her! Now go! Come back a better woo-er!

(CELIA shoves ORLANDO off stage; ORLANDO re-enters)

ORLANDO: My dear, Rosalind...

ROSALIND: *(interrupting)* Better... Now, come, woo me, woo me.

ORLANDO: Ok... I love you.

ROSALIND: *(mocking ORLANDO)* I love you... blah, blah, blah... you do not love. Show me LOVE!

ORLANDO: I die for love and I would die for you!

ROSALIND: Better. But, you saw what happened to Romeo & Juliet, dying for love may not be the best thing. I got it! Aliena, act as a priest and marry us!

CELIA: *(shocked)* What?!

ROSALIND: Priest, you know... marriage! Just do it!

CELIA: Okey-dokey. *(they hold hands)* Will you, Orlando, have to wife this Rosalind?

ORLANDO: I will. I take thee, Rosalind, for a wife.

ROSALIND: *(feeling love-struck)* Wow. Ok, you're doing great!

ORLANDO: But, will my Rosalind do so?

ROSALIND: By my life, she will do as I do! *(to audience)* Really, she will!

ORLANDO: O, but she is wise!

ROSALIND: *(to audience)* Very true! *(to ORLANDO)* Now, get out of here and don't be late again!

ORLANDO: Aye, sweet Rosalind. Adieu! *(exits)*

CELIA: Wow, you really got him in shape!

ROSALIND: *(sighs heavily)* I know...

CELIA: *(pulling ROSALIND offstage)* Come on crazy Cupid.

(ALL exit)

ACT 4 SCENE 2

(enter AUDREY and TOUCHSTONE)

TOUCHSTONE: Hey, you're cute.

AUDREY: Ahhh... thanks!

TOUCHSTONE: I have an idea, let's get married!

AUDREY: You're funny.

TOUCHSTONE: I know. Listen, you're in the play because, well... they thought it would be ironic for me to fall in love.

AUDREY: Ah, you're so romantic, too! Ok. By the way, the name's Audrey.

TOUCHSTONE: Sweet! I'm Touchstone!

(they hold hands and exit)

ACT 4 SCENE 3

(enter ROSALIND [Ganymede] and CELIA [Aliena])

ROSALIND: He's late again, this time TWO hours! What a nincompoop! Why do I love him so?

CELIA: You're putting too much pressure on him. Look who comes here.

(enter SILVIUS)

SILVIUS: Ganymede, Phebe wrote this letter for me to give to you.

ROSALIND: *(reading letter)* Wow, she's rude.

SILVIUS: But, I love her.

ROSALIND: You are a fool.

SILVIUS: True. But I still love her.

ROSALIND: Listen, it says she likes Ganymede.

SILVIUS: Isn't that you?

ROSALIND: Ahhh, yeah. I mean she likes me. So, tell her that if she loves me, that I will never love her unless she loves you.

SILVIUS: Huh?

ROSALIND: Exactly! Now go!

(CELIA shoves SILVIUS off stage who is very confused)

CELIA: Alas, poor shepherd.

(enter OLIVER)

OLIVER: I'm looking for a young guy and a... *(suddenly seeing CELIA's beauty)* BEAUTIFUL maiden... wow... Is this you?

CELIA: We are.

OLIVER: I bring a message from Orlando.

ROSALIND: This better be good.

OLIVER: Oh, it is! I was asleep in the forest when a green and gilded snake was about to attack me, and he saved me!

ROSALIND: That's it?

OLIVER: No! It gets better... THEN a lioness was lurking nearby about to eat me, and he fought the lioness to save me!

ROSALIND: Ok, that's better...

OLIVER: AND... he did this for me, HIS BROTHER, who kept trying to kill him! He's such a good person and I'm a dork! See... his blood!

(OLIVER hands bloody handkerchief to ROSALIND)

ROSALIND: Oh, Orlando! *(swoons)*

CELIA: How now, Ganymede!

OLIVER: Hmmm... I wonder why he did that? Hey, wake up... it's just blood. You lack a man's heart.

ROSALIND: Ahhh... I was acting the part of Rosalind for Orlando's sake... yeah!

OLIVER: Yeah, ok. I'll let him know that... *(aside)* strange.

(ALL exit)

ACT 5 SCENE 1

(enter OLIVER and ORLANDO)

OLIVER: Hey brother, I love Aliena and we are getting married!

ORLANDO: WHAT? You two literally met a minute ago.

OLIVER: Right?! I took one look at her and BAM, the shepherd's life for me!

ORLANDO: Ok, well, let your wedding be tomorrow.

OLIVER: Sweet! And I haven't seen her for like, 2 minutes, so... later!

(OLIVER exits; enter ROSALIND [Ganymede])

ORLANDO: *(to audience)* Oh look, here comes my "Rosalind".

ROSALIND: Hey, why do you look so sad.

ORLANDO: My brother's happiness tomorrow will match my sadness. I long for Rosalind.

ROSALIND: Okay, I've been keeping this a secret, but... I am a magician!

ORLANDO: I'm sorry, what?

ROSALIND: Listen, if you do love Rosalind, then tomorrow, at your brother's wedding, shall you marry her!

ORLANDO: How?!

(enter PHEBE and SILVIUS)

PHEBE: *(to ROSALIND)* Ganymede, I love you.

SILVIUS: Phebe, I love you.

ORLANDO: *(to no one)* Rosalind, I love you.

ROSALIND: Who do you speak to?

ORLANDO: To her that is not here.

ROSALIND: Ok, you love fools, all of you meet here tomorrow and I promise you, you will marry the one you love!

PHEBE: Wait, how do you know this?

ROSALIND: Easy, it's a Shakespeare comedy, and EVERYONE gets married at the end of those!

ALL: Ohhhh...

(ALL exit)

ACT 5 SCENE 2

(enter TOUCHSTONE and AUDREY)

TOUCHSTONE: The fool doth think he is wise, but the wise man knows himself to be a fool.

AUDREY: You are so smart and funny!

TOUCHSTONE: I know.

AUDREY: Hey, everyone else is getting married tomorrow. Do you want to?

TOUCHSTONE: And you are brilliant! Yes!

AUDREY: SWEET!!!

(ALL exit)

ACT 5 SCENE 3

(enter DUKE SENIOR, OLIVER, ORLANDO, SILVIUS, PHEBE, CELIA [Aliena], and ROSALIND [Ganymede])

DUKE S: *(to ORLANDO)* Do you believe the boy can do all that he hath promised?

ORLANDO: If it means I have to believe in magic, then yes!

ROSALIND: Ok, everyone, let's refresh! If I bring Rosalind, you'll marry her?

ORLANDO: Yep!

ROSALIND: And you'll marry me, if I be willing? But, if you do refuse, you'll marry this most faithful shepherd?

PHEBE: Refuse you? Suuure... I'll marry anyone you want me to! I'll even marry that random audience member right there!

ROSALIND: Good. And you're good with this, right?

SILVIUS: Oh, yeah!

ROSALIND: Great! Give us a minute.

(exit ROSALIND and CELIA)

DUKE S: Have you noticed that Ganymede sure looks a lot like Rosalind?

OLIVER: Right? He's so lucky to find such a doppelganger!

(enter TOUCHSTONE and AUDREY)

TOUCHSTONE: Are we late?

DUKE S: Nope, the party's just getting started!

AUDREY: Sweet! *(pointing at herself)* Look how lucky he got!

(enter HYMEN, ROSALIND [Ganymede], and CELIA as herself)

ROSALIND: Look who I brought! *(presenting CELIA to OLIVER)*

OLIVER: *(noticing CELIA)* Wow! You clean up well!

CELIA: Yep! And we brought the God of Love, literally!

OLIVER: Whoa, you really did. Was he just randomly wandering through the woods?

CELIA: Yep!

ROSALIND: And I brought Rosalind! *(removes disguise)*

DUKE S: My daughter!

ORLANDO: My Rosalind!

PHEBE: My gosh, I have to marry the shepherd now?!

SILVIUS: Yes!

ROSALIND: See, I told you. Magic!

HYMEN: You eight must take hands. *(to PHEBE)* Even you.

PHEBE: Ugh. Fine!

HYMEN: *(claps his hands)* OK, you're all married! Time to party!

ALL: Yeah! *(ALL exit except ROSALIND)*

EPILOGUE

ROSALIND: Ok, we're done here. Why don't you go grab your loved ones and party too! Bye!

THE END

PRONUNCIATION KEY

ROSALIND: RAH-za-lind
GANYMEDE: GAN-uh-meed
CELIA: SEAL-ya
ALIENA: ALIEN-a
JAQUES: JAY-queez
CORIN: CORE-in
AMIENS: AY-mee-unz
COZ: cuz
LIEGE: leej

Special Thanks

Special thanks to Bridget and Jerry's theatre classes from the Houston Independent School District. Your kids ALWAYS have great ideas!

Bradley, I appreciate you taking the time to dive into this text and give some great constructive feedback and creative ideas.

A BIG SHOUT OUT to my Facebook and Twitter followers. Your constructive criticism and candid feedback made this cover so much more awesome! Specific thanks to Dave Coonan, Debba Rofheart, Leslie Nelson, Bonnie Adams, Charity Ford, Kayla Thompson, Alva Sachs, Mia Lopez, and Kimberly Gatto!!!

More special thanks to Khara C. Barnhart, Suzy Newman, Debba (you burped? LOL!), Amanda Thayer, Jean, Angi Herrick, Royce, Marian, and Lisa M! As always, your feedback helps these kids get a much richer experience with Shakespeare!

-Brendan

Sneak Peeks at other Playing With Plays books:

Sneak peek of
TREASURE ISLAND
for Kids

(enter JIM, TRELAWNEY, and DOCTOR; enter CAPTAIN SMOLLETT from the other side of the stage)

TRELAWNEY: Hello Captain. Are we all shipshape and seaworthy?

CAPTAIN: Trelawney, I don't know what you're thinking, but I don't like this cruise; and I don't like the men.

TRELAWNEY: *(very angry)* Perhaps you don't like the ship?

CAPTAIN: Nope, I said it short and sweet.

DOCTOR: What? Why?

CAPTAIN: Because I heard we are going on a treasure hunt and the coordinates of the island are: *(whispers to DOCTOR)*

DOCTOR: Wow! That's exactly right!

CAPTAIN: There's been too much blabbing already.

DOCTOR: Right! But, I doubt ANYTHING will go wrong!

CAPTAIN: Fine. Let's sail!

(ALL exit)

Act 2 Scene 3

(enter JIM, SILVER, and various other pirates)

SILVER: Ay, ay, mates. You know the song: Fifteen men on the dead man's chest.

ALL PIRATES: Yo-ho-ho and a bottle of rum!

(PIRATES slowly exit)

JIM: *(to the audience)* So, the Hispaniola had begun her voyage to the Isle of Treasure. As for Long John, well, he still is the nicest cook...

SILVER: Do you want a sandwich?

JIM: That would be great, thanks Long John! *(SILVER exits; JIM addresses audience)* As you can see, Long John is a swell guy! Until...

(JIM hides in the corner)

Act 2 Scene 4

(enter SILVER and OTHER PIRATES)

JIM: *(to audience)* I overheard Long John talking to the rest of the pirates.

SILVER: Listen here you, Scallywags! I was with Captain Flint when he hid this treasure. And those cowards have the map. Follow my directions, and no killing, yet. Clear?

DICK: Clear.

SILVER: But, when we do kill them, I claim Trelawney. And remember, dead men don't bite.

GEORGE: Ay, ay, Long John!

(ALL exit but JIM)

JIM: *(to audience)* Oh no! Long John Silver IS the one-legged man that Billy Bones warned me about! I have to tell the others!

(JIM runs offstage)

Sneak peek of
KING LEAR
for Kids
ACT 1 SCENE 1
KING LEAR's palace

(enter FOOL entertaining the audience with jokes, dancing, juggling, Hula Hooping... whatever the actor's skill may be; enter KENT)

KENT: Hey, Fool!

FOOL: What did you call me?!

KENT: I called you Fool.

FOOL: That's my name, don't wear it out! *(to audience)* Seriously, that's my name in the play!

(enter LEAR, CORNWALL, ALBANY, GONERIL, REGAN, and CORDELIA)

LEAR: The lords of France and Burgundy are outside. They both want to marry you, Cordelia.

ALL: Ooooooo!

LEAR: *(to audience)* Between you and me she IS my favorite child! *(to the girls)* Daughters, I need to talk to you about something. It's a really big deal.

GONERIL & REGAN: Did you buy us presents?

LEAR: This is even better than presents!

GONERIL & REGAN: Goody, goody!!!

CORDELIA: Father, your love is enough for me.

LEAR: Give me the map there, Kent. Girls, I'm tired. I've made a decision: Know that we - and by 'we' I mean 'me' - have divided in three our kingdom...

KENT: Whoa! Sir, dividing the kingdom may cause chaos! People could die!

FOOL: Well, this IS a tragedy...

LEAR: You worry too much, Kent. I'm giving it to my daughters so their husbands can be rich and powerful... like me!

CORNWALL & ALBANY: Sweet!

GONERIL & REGAN: Wait... what?

CORDELIA: This is olden times. That means that everything we own belongs to our husbands.

GONERIL & REGAN: Olden times stink!

CORDELIA: Truth.

LEAR: So, my daughters, tell your daddy how much you love him. Goneril, our eldest-born, speak first.

GONERIL: Sir, I love you more than words can say! More than outer space, puppies and cotton candy! I love you more than any child has ever loved a father in the history of the entire world, dearest Pops!

CORDELIA: *(to audience)* Holy moly! Surely, he won't be fooled by that. *(to self)* Love, and be silent.

LEAR: Thanks, sweetie! I'm giving you this big chunk of the kingdom here. What says our second daughter, Our dearest Regan, wife to Cornwall? Speak.

REGAN: What she said, Daddy... times a thousand!

CORDELIA: *(to audience)* What?! I love my father more than either of them. But I can't express it in words. My love's more richer than my tongue.

LEAR: Wow, Regan! You get this big hunk of the kingdom. Cordelia, what can you tell me to get this giant piece of kingdom as your own? Speak.

CORDELIA: Nothing, my lord.

LEAR: Nothing?!?

CORDELIA: Nothing.

LEAR: Come on, now. Nothing will come of nothing.

CORDELIA: I love you as a daughter loves her father.

LEAR: Try a little, harder, sweetie!

CORDELIA: Why are my sisters married if they give you all their love?

LEAR: How did you get so mean?

CORDELIA: Father, I will not insult you by telling you my love is like... as big as a whale.

LEAR: *(getting mad)* Fine. I'll split your share between your sisters.

REGAN, GONERIL, & CORNWALL: Yessss!

KENT: Whoa! Let's all just calm down a minute!

LEAR: Peace, Kent! You don't want to mess with me right now. I told you she was my favorite...

GONERIL & REGAN: What!?

LEAR: ...and she can't even tell me she loves me more than a whale? Nope. Now I'm mad.

KENT: Royal Lear, really...

LEAR: Kent, I'm pretty emotional right now! You better not try to talk me out of this...

KENT: Sir, you're acting ... insane.

Sneak peek of
FRANKENSTEIN
for Kids
ACT 1 SCENE 1

(enter WALDMAN and VICTOR)

WALDMAN: Victor! Come in! You look so tired.

VICTOR: I'm fine, Professor Waldman! I've been working on an experiment. There's so much to be done.

WALDMAN: You remind me of myself as a young student! So few of us are willing to give our right arms for science!

VICTOR: You have no idea! *(to audience)* I will solve the mysteries of creation! *(laughs madly)*

WALDMAN: Pardon me?

VICTOR: I said...ahhh... I need a vacation! Gotta go back to work. Excuse me! *(VICTOR exits)*

WALDMAN: Strange kid.

(WALDMAN exits; VICTOR pops back on stage and addresses audience)

VICTOR: He'd think I'm mad if I told him! I've figured out how to make dead things live again! *(laughs madly, exits and returns with arms and legs)* I've been through dozens of graves and hospitals. Finally, I have everything I need!

(exits, laughing madly)

ACT 1 SCENE 2

(MONSTER is laying under a sheet; VICTOR enters)

VICTOR: *(to audience)* I see by your eagerness that you expect to see how it's done. Ha! If I showed you, you'd be...SHOCKED! Time to become the world's first bodybuilder! *(VICTOR laughs madly as he raises the sheet to hide himself and MONSTER)* To bolt or not to bolt, THAT is the question! *(there's a clap of thunder, then VICTOR yanks away sheet)*

MONSTER: *(sits up in monster voice)* GRR!!! GRR!!!

VICTOR: It's alive! It's alive!! IT'S ALIVE!!!

MONSTER: You never said that in the book!

VICTOR: I know but, it's more fun to say...IT'S ALIVE!

MONSTER: *(MONSTER takes one step towards VICTOR)* GRR!!!

VICTOR: OK!!! AAGH!!! Monster! *(screams and runs to other side of stage)*

MONSTER: Now THAT'S what you said in the book! ARGHHH!!!

(VICTOR runs away screaming, MONSTER takes the sheet and wears it like a cloak, exits)

ABOUT THE AUTHOR

BRENDAN P. KELSO came to writing modified Shakespeare scripts when he was taking time off from work to be at home with his newly born son. "It just grew from there". Within months, he was being asked to offer classes in various locations and acting organizations along the Central Coast of California. Originally employed as an engineer, Brendan never thought about writing. However, his unique personality, humor, and love for engaging the kids with The Bard has led him to leave the engineering world and pursue writing as a new adventure in life! He has always believed, "the best way to learn is to have fun!" Brendan makes his home on the Central Coast of California and loves to spend time with his wife and kids.

CAST AUTOGRAPHS

Made in United States
North Haven, CT
01 September 2022

23514733R00059